THE TIDE
D-DAY INVASION
TURNS

MURRAY • ELSON • WILLIAMS

First published in Great Britain in 2007 by Osprey Publishing,
Midland House, West Way, Botley, Oxford OX2 0PH, UK
443 Park Avenue South, New York, NY 10016, USA

A CIP catalog record for this book is available from the British Library

ISBN 978 1 84603 056 7

Page layout by Osprey Publishing
Map by The Map Studio
Originated by United Graphics Pte Ltd, Singapore
Printed in China through Bookbuilders

07 08 09 10 11   10 9 8 7 6 5 4 3 2 1

FOR A CATALOG OF ALL BOOKS PUBLISHED BY OSPREY MILITARY AND AVIATION
PLEASE CONTACT:

NORTH AMERICA
Osprey Direct, c/o Random House Distribution Center, 400 Hahn Road,
Westminster, MD 21157
E-mail: info@ospreydirect.com

ALL OTHER REGIONS
Osprey Direct UK, P.O. Box 140 Wellingborough, Northants, NN8 2FA, UK
E-mail: info@ospreydirect.co.uk

www.ospreypublishing.com

CONTENTS

WHO'S WHO

General Dwight D. Eisenhower (1890–1969) was Commander-in-Chief of SHAEF (Supreme Headquarters Allied Expeditionary Force) and in charge of all Allied troops in the European Theater. After the war, he was twice elected President of the United States.

Field Marshall Erwin Rommel (1891–1944) was relieved from command of the famed "Afrika Korps" before their final defeat in North Africa. He was transferred to France where he was tasked with building coastal defenses against the anticipated Allied Invasion.

Field Marshall Bernard Law Montgomery (1887–1976) was commander of the British Eight Army—the famous "Desert Rats" who defeated Rommel in North Africa. After this success, he was appointed to be Eisenhower's chief deputy in planning Operation *Overlord*.

Adolf Hitler (1889–1945) was leader of Germany and commander of German forces from 1944. Convinced of his divine right to lead Germany to power over all, Hitler began his conquering of Europe in Poland in 1939.

WORLD WAR 2
1939 – 1945

Even after World War 1 (1914–1919), there were strong hostilities between many nations. The United States worked to build good relations with other countries to avoid fighting another war.

However, other nations were becoming aggressive toward their neighbors. In 1936, Italy invaded Ethiopia. Japan attacked China in 1937. In 1938, Germany took control of Austria and Czechoslovakia.

In 1939, Germany invaded Poland. France and England responded by declaring war on Germany. The United States had avoided fighting in the growing worldwide conflict, but on December 7, 1941, Japan attacked the U.S. naval base at Pearl Harbor, Hawaii. America was at war.

For the next four years, the United States and its allies fought Germany and the other Axis forces on land, sea, and in the air. One of the most decisive campaigns was the D-Day invasion, in 1944, the beginning of the Allies' plan to take back Europe. Its outcome was so important that many historians call this campaign the turning point of the war. ■

FIGHTING BACK

After the British Expeditionary Force had been evacuated from the European mainland in 1940, the German Army had gained control of the bulk of Western Europe. From that time forward, all operations against the Nazis had been limited to areas away from the German homeland.

British, and later, American forces were both confined to operations in Northern Africa and, after a seaborne assault, Crete, Sicily, and finally, Italy.

In the East, the Russians were fighting against Hitler's main forces practically on their own.

It was clear that it would be necessary to open a second front in Europe if only to reduce the pressure on the Russians.

▲

The North coast of France was dotted with concrete gun fortifications. The Germans were heavily sheltered when firing the guns, such as shown here, and this proved deadly for the Allies on D-Day. (NARA)

Planning for an invasion began as early as 1943 and, after eliminating the option of going through the Balkans or continuing through Italy, it was agreed that an attack upon Northern France offered the best

Planning for the invasion was a massive undertaking. Every available space in England, UK, was used to store vehicles, such as these Cromwell and Churchill tanks, and the equipment needed for the attack. (IWM)

chance of success—and the shortest route to the German homeland.

The Americans, at first, wanted to stage two amphibious assaults—one on Northwestern France, and a second along the French Mediterranean. However, it was decided that there just weren't enough men and equipment to make this work.

They then looked at the Pas de Calais— across the narrowest point of the English Channel. It had the advantage of a good port and offered the shortest route into Germany—through the Low Countries. However, it was also the most obvious target and the one the Germans were working hard to secure and protect.

The next most likely place was Normandy. The Bay of Seine offered some shelter from bad weather and there were enough beaches that were suitable for assault by sea. Normandy was also probably less heavily defended than Calais.

Normandy did not have any large ports but the British had already begun to develop an artificial harbor that would be enough to move men and machines until a more substantial port could be seized.

The first draft of the "Overlord" plan was completed in July 1943 and quickly approved by the combined Allied Chiefs of Staff. Full planning began at once.

Senior American commanders on D-Day were, left to right, LtGen Omar Bradley, MajGen Leonard Gerow, Gen Dwight Eisenhower and Gen J. Lawson Collins. (NARA)

▼

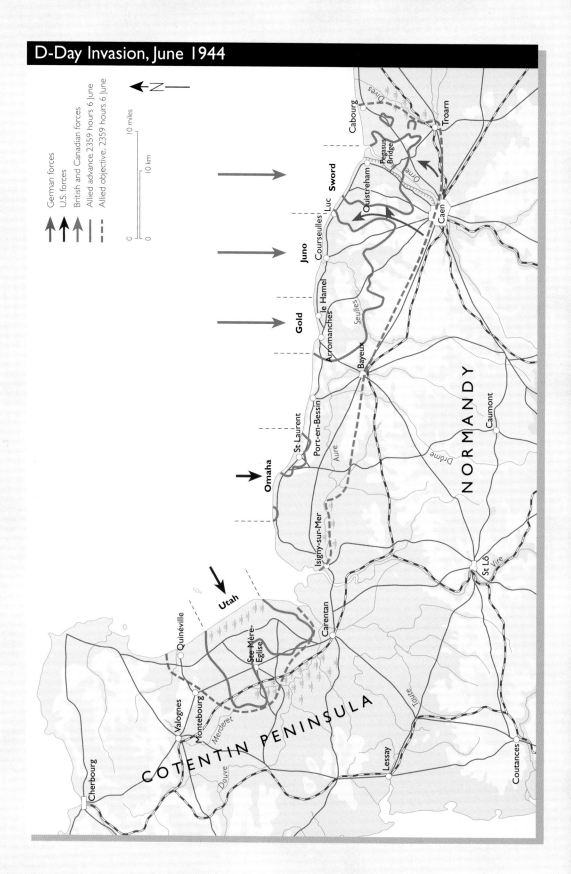

D-Day Invasion, June 1944

German forces
U.S. forces
British and Canadian forces
Allied advance, 2359 hours 6 June
Allied objective, 2359 hours 6 June

10 miles
10 km

Cabourg
Dives
Troarn
Pegasus Bridge
Sword
Ouistreham
Orne
Luc
Caen
Juno
Courseulles
le Hamel
Gold
Seulles
Arromanches
Bayeux
NORMANDY
Caumont
St Laurent
Port-en-Bessin
Aure
Omaha
Drôme
Isigny-sur-Mer
St Lô
Vire
Utah
Carentan
Quinéville
Ste-Mère-Eglise
Valognes
Montebourg
Merderet
COTENTIN PENINSULA
Taute
Lessay
Cherbourg
Douve
Coutances

THE ALLIES ARE COMING

The Germans were aware that an Allied invasion of France was coming. Field Marshall Erwin Rommel had been given command of the French beaches in late 1943 and took action to fortify and protect all the beaches, to stop any invasion before the enemy could gain a foothold.

Limited resources slowed work and by the middle of 1944, much remained to be done. Worse, the Allies had made a concerted effort to disrupt the German meteorology service. This meant that the German commanders had incomplete weather information and thought the weather would be too poor for an invasion in early June.

Meanwhile, General Eisenhower, after cancelling June 5 as the invasion date, decided to move forward on June 6. As the Allies had complete weather information, he knew that he would have a few days of decent weather in which to mount his assaults.

The Allied invasion now started with the deployment of airborne elements. The American 82nd and 101st Divisions and the British 6th and 1st Parachute Regiments were sent into France on the night of 5 July—their job was to secure the battlefield by blowing up bridges over rivers on enemy approach roads, and hold key bridges to allow troops from the seaborne invasion force access inland once they were off the beaches.

Meanwhile, the largest Allied fleet ever assembled began to disembark its troops on beaches off the coast of France.

LEFT Allied forces landed on the French coast on five beaches, Utah, Omaha, Gold, Juno and Sword. The plan was simple—defeat the Axis forces, and take back Europe.

▲

A scene from Omaha Beach on the first morning of the Allied invasion. The Allies had used every available resource to make the attack a success. (NARA)

Warships began a fierce bombardment of German positions, joined by aircraft. Despite this, German fire and pre-set obstacles took their toll on the seaborne troops. Many died without ever reaching the beaches and, once ashore, many more found themselves trapped by heavy German fire.

Omaha Beach was the worst. Tank support should have been provided by DD (Dual Drive) tanks sent in along with the troops. However, most of the tanks sank in the heavy seas. The Americans found themselves under continuous fire and the attack at Omaha was in doubt. Success of the reinforcements and good leadership on the beach managed to save them and they finally made a breakthrough to higher ground.

Meanwhile, landings at Sword, Gold, Juno, and Utah Beaches were successful.

German opposition was light and allowed the Allies to break through the existing defenses and, by the end of the day, begin to move inland, hooking up with airborne units as they moved.

A beachhead had been established—and the Allies were firmly launched in their crusade to reconquer Western Europe.

THE D-DAY INVASION:
THE LIBERATION OF EUROPE BEGINS

LATE SPRING, 1944. THE GERMAN ARMY IS LOSING ITS GRIP ON WESTERN EUROPE AS ALLIED ARMIES TAKE COMMAND IN NORTH AFRICA AND ITALY.

GERMAN FIELD MARSHALL ERWIN ROMMEL HAS BEEN GIVEN RESPONSIBILITY FOR THE DEFENSE OF THE ATLANTIC COAST.

HE KNOWS THAT IF GIVEN TIME HE CAN MAKE AN ALLIED INVASION DIFFICULT -- PERHAPS IMPOSSIBLE.

IF GIVEN ENOUGH TIME...

THE GERMANS KNOW THAT THE ALLIES HAVE NEVER MOUNTED AN INVASION IN BAD WEATHER. AND THE WEATHER THIS JUNE HAS BEEN VERY BAD...

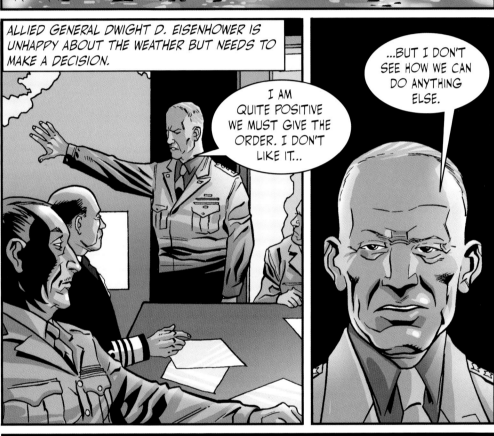

ALLIED GENERAL DWIGHT D. EISENHOWER IS UNHAPPY ABOUT THE WEATHER BUT NEEDS TO MAKE A DECISION.

I AM QUITE POSITIVE WE MUST GIVE THE ORDER. I DON'T LIKE IT...

...BUT I DON'T SEE HOW WE CAN DO ANYTHING ELSE.

NIGHT. JUNE 5, 1944...

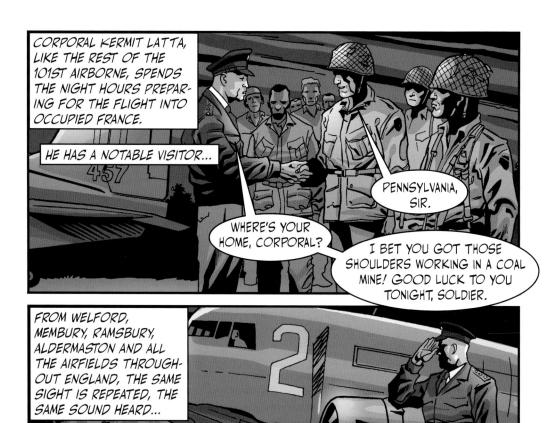

CORPORAL KERMIT LATTA, LIKE THE REST OF THE 101ST AIRBORNE, SPENDS THE NIGHT HOURS PREPARING FOR THE FLIGHT INTO OCCUPIED FRANCE.

HE HAS A NOTABLE VISITOR...

WHERE'S YOUR HOME, CORPORAL?

PENNSYLVANIA, SIR.

I BET YOU GOT THOSE SHOULDERS WORKING IN A COAL MINE! GOOD LUCK TO YOU TONIGHT, SOLDIER.

FROM WELFORD, MEMBURY, RAMSBURY, ALDERMASTON AND ALL THE AIRFIELDS THROUGHOUT ENGLAND, THE SAME SIGHT IS REPEATED, THE SAME SOUND HEARD...

THE AIRBORNE TROOPS ARE ON THEIR WAY...

THEIR JOB IS TO SECURE BRIDGES, BLOCK ROADS, AND STOP GERMAN REINFORCEMENTS FROM REACHING THE BEACHES.

THEY ARE THE VERY TIP OF THE ALLIED SPEARHEAD.

THE FIRST ACTION IS TO BE BY A BRITISH GLIDER FORCE.

SURPRISE IS VITAL IF THEY ARE TO COMPLETE THEIR JOB.

MAJOR JOHN HOWARD WATCHES AS HIS GLIDER APPROACHES THE LANDING ZONE (LZ). HIS DIFFICULT TASK IS TO TAKE AND HOLD THE TWO BRIDGES OVER THE LORNE RIVER AND CAEN CANAL BEHIND ENEMY LINES.

HERE WE GO, MEN!

HOWARD KNOWS THAT IF THE BRIDGES CAN BE HELD, GERMAN REINFORCEMENTS WILL BE PREVENTED FROM REACHING THE CANADIAN AND BRITISH BEACH INVASIONS.

HE ALSO KNOWS HE HAS ONLY ONE COMPANY OF MEN TO DO IT WITH.

COME ON, LADS!

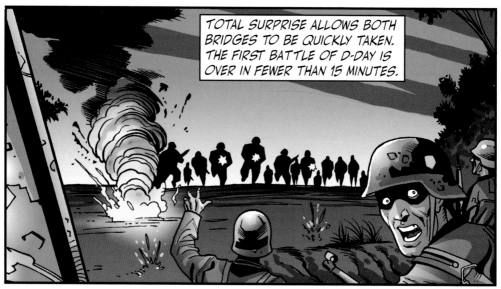

TOTAL SURPRISE ALLOWS BOTH BRIDGES TO BE QUICKLY TAKEN. THE FIRST BATTLE OF D-DAY IS OVER IN FEWER THAN 15 MINUTES.

HOWARD ORDERS HIS 150 MEN TO HOLD THE BRIDGE UNTIL THEY ARE RELIEVED.

...NO MATTER HOW LONG THAT MAY TAKE.

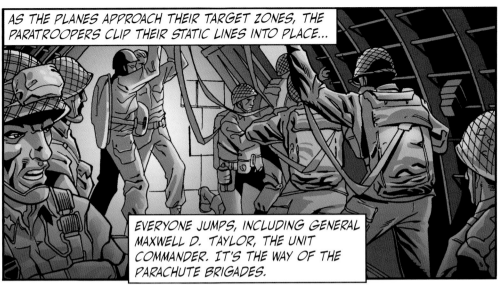

AS THE PLANES APPROACH THEIR TARGET ZONES, THE PARATROOPERS CLIP THEIR STATIC LINES INTO PLACE...

EVERYONE JUMPS, INCLUDING GENERAL MAXWELL D. TAYLOR, THE UNIT COMMANDER. IT'S THE WAY OF THE PARACHUTE BRIGADES.

THEN THE UNEXPECTED HAPPENS...

A BANK OF CLOUDS SUDDENLY APPEARS OVER THE FINAL APPROACH ROUTE...

THE PILOTS HAVE TO ACT QUICKLY TO AVOID COLLISIONS...

OOOFH!

AAARGH!

13

THE UNEXPECTED CLOUDS HAVE BROKEN UP THE AIR FORMATIONS...

WE'RE THERE! GO, GO, GO!

... A FACT UNKNOWN TO THE TROOPS JUMPING INTO BATTLE.

MEN ARE LOST IN THE WATER AS THEY FALL INTO FLOODED AREAS.

NORMANDY MARSH-LAND HAD BEEN FLOODED BY THE GERMANS.

UNNNFFFF!

GET MOVING, MEN!

OTHERS LAND SAFELY, AND ARE QUICKLY GATHERED INTO UNITS BY THEIR OFFICERS.

ON THE GROUND, THE SURVIVING PARATROOPS OF THE 101ST AIRBORNE GO TO WORK. LT. TURNER TURNBULL ORGANIZES A DEFENSE OF THE ROAD THROUGH NEUVILLE...

...WHILE CAPTAIN RICHARD WINTERS AND HIS MEN TAKE ON A HIDDEN BATTERY OF GERMAN CANNON.

ALL OVER THE COTENTIN PENINSULA, AIRBORNE TROOPS -- OUTNUMBERED, OUTGUNNED, AND ALONE -- PREPARE TO HOLD THEIR GROUND.

THE FIRST LIGHT OF DAWN OVER OMAHA BEACH...

GERMAN MAJOR WERNER PLUSKAT HAS BEEN AT HIS POST SINCE THE FIRST REPORTS OF PARACHUTE LANDINGS WERE RELAYED TO HIS HEADQUARTERS.

HE IS COLD, TIRED, AND UNSURE OF WHAT IS REALLY HAPPENING.

UNTIL...

MEIN GOTT!*

* OH MY GOD!

MAJOR PLUSKAT IS A GOOD SOLDIER, BUT IN THIS MOMENT HE KNOWS THIS IS THE END OF THE WAR FOR GERMANY.

IT IS THE INVASION! TEN THOUSAND SHIPS!

AS THE GERMANS RUSH TO THEIR DEFENSES, OFF THE SHORES OF NORMANDY...

OPEN FIRE!

THE WARSHIPS OF THE INVASION FLEET OPEN FIRE. HUNDREDS OF SHELLS SCREAM OVER THE WATER...

...HITTING PRE-SELECTED TARGETS ALL ALONG THE NORMANDY BEACHHEAD.

ALLIED AIRCRAFT NOW BEGIN AN ASSAULT ON THEIR TARGET -- THE GERMAN GUNS TRAINED ON OMAHA BEACH.

CAPTAIN ALLEN W. STEPHENS IS FLYING HIS TWENTY-FIRST MISSION. HE IS AWED BY THE NUMBER OF SHIPS AND MEN HE SEES BELOW.

BUT ONCE OVER THE BEACH, HE AND HIS CREW CANNOT SEE THEIR TARGETS. RELUCTANTLY, THEY FLY FURTHER INLAND TO DROP THEIR BOMBS -- LEAVING THE GERMAN COASTAL GUNS UNTOUCHED.

AS THE BARRAGE CONTINUES, AMERICAN TROOPS HEAD FOR UTAH AND OMAHA BEACHES.

THE BOMBARDMENT FROM THE "SEA WALL*" WHISTLES OVER THEIR HEADS AS AIRCRAFT MAKE THEIR FINAL ATTACKS ON THE FRENCH MAINLAND.

THE NOISE IS DEAFENING.

* THE SEA WALL WAS A BARRIER BUILT BY THE GERMANS. IT WAS MADE OF WOODEN LOGS AND WAS BETWEEN 2 AND 3 FEET HIGH.

STAFF SERGEANT ALFRED EIGENBERG, AN ARMY MEDIC, HAS FEARED THAT HE WOULD GET SEASICK...

...BUT THE NEED TO BAIL OUT THE BOAT PUSHES EVERYTHING ELSE OUT OF HIS MIND.

SOME MEN IN OTHER LANDING CRAFT DON'T RESPOND AS QUICKLY. THEY DIE IN SIGHT OF THE BEACH -- WITHOUT FIRING A SHOT.

THE 741ST TANK BATTALION IS ASSIGNED TO SUPPORT THE LANDINGS ON OMAHA BEACH.

BUT THE WATER IS ROUGHER THAN ANTICIPATED, AND THE HIGH SURF POUNDS THE TANKS AS SOON AS THEY ENTER THE WATER.

WAVES TEAR THROUGH THE TANKS' CANVAS WATER WINGS, BREAKING SUPPORT BEAMS AND FLOODING ENGINES.

THOSE TANKS SINK AND PULL THEIR CREWS DOWN UNDER THE WATER.

COMMANDERS, OUT OF CONTACT AND UNAWARE THAT THEY HAVE LOST THEIR ARMOR SUPPORT, CONTINUE WITH THE OMAHA BEACH LANDINGS...

LANDING CRAFT GET AS CLOSE TO THE BEACH AS THEY CAN -- UNTIL THEY MEET THE OBSTACLES ERECTED BY THE GERMANS.

THE MEN DO WHAT THEY HAVE BEEN TRAINED TO DO. THEY MOVE FORWARD, CROUCH, AND FIRE.

UNFORTUNATELY, THERE IS NOTHING FOR THEM TO FIRE AT!

TARGETS ARE HARD TO FIND, AND IT'S A STRUGGLE TO STAY UPRIGHT.

21

DESPERATE SOLDIERS ABANDON THEIR EQUIPMENT AS THEY TRY TO REACH THE BEACH.

SGT. TOM VALENCE, A RIFLE SERGEANT IN A-COMPANY OF THE 116TH INFANTRY, IS HIT IN THE HAND AS HE LEAVES HIS BOAT.

HE TRIES TO SHOOT BACK BUT HIS RIFLE WILL NOT WORK.

SGT. VALENCE KEEPS MOVING FORWARD...

HE KNOWS IT IS IMPOSSIBLE TO KNOCK OUT A GERMAN CONCRETE EMPLACEMENT WITH A 30-CALIBER RIFLE -- BUT HE IS DETERMINED TO FIGHT.

HE IS HIT AGAIN, AND AGAIN...

WOUNDED AND EXHAUSTED, VALENCE FINALLY FINDS SHELTER -- ONE LIVE BODY AMONG MANY DEAD ONES.

THE STORY IS THE SAME ALONG THE LENGTH OF OMAHA BEACH...

THE DROPPING OF RAMPS SEEMS A SIGNAL FOR CONCENTRATED AND MURDEROUS GERMAN MACHINE-GUN FIRE.

ALL ALONG THE LENGTH OF OMAHA BEACH, OTHER ALLIED TROOPS LIE, IN THE HUNDREDS, HUDDLED BEHIND WHAT COVER THEY CAN FIND...

...AND WAIT.

AS THE AMERICANS LIE PINNED DOWN BY THE SEVERE FIRE ON OMAHA BEACH, THE CANADIAN DIVISION BEGINS ITS ASSAULT ON JUNO BEACH.

ROUGH SEAS HAVE DELAYED THE CANADIANS' LANDINGS LONG ENOUGH FOR THE TIDE TO DROP -- REVEALING THE GERMAN TRAPS AWAITING THE INVADERS OF THE NORMANDY COAST...

...MINES, CONTACT-FUSED SHELLS, AND ALL MANNER OF DEATH TRAPS.

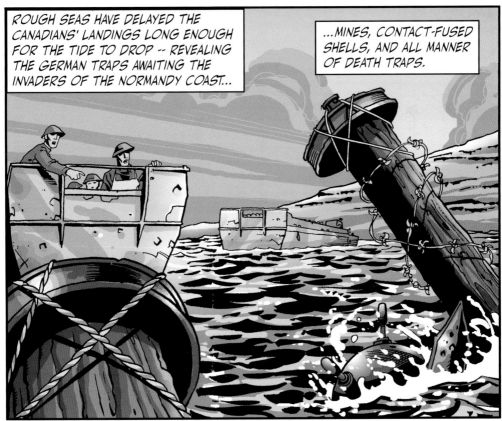

...TRAPS THAT CANNOT BE AVOIDED.

COME ON, MEN!

BUT EVEN WHEN THEIR LANDING CRAFT ARE DAMAGED OR SUNK, MOST OF THE INFANTRY IS ABLE TO STRUGGLE ASHORE.

AND UNLIKE OMAHA BEACH, THEIR ARMOR SUPPORT IS WAITING FOR THEM.

WITH THE EASE BORN OF LONG PRACTICE, THE CANADIANS BEGIN THEIR ASSAULT.

THE GERMANS PREPARE THEIR OWN FIRE, KNOWING THEY HAVE ONLY A FEW MINUTES TO BLUNT THE LANDING OR BE KILLED.

THE REGINA RIFLE REGIMENT HAS BEEN ASSIGNED TO TAKE THE VILLAGE OF COURSECULLES, THE STRONGEST POINT IN THE AREA. THE VILLAGE AND ITS HARBOR HAVE BEEN DIVIDED INTO 12 SECTORS, EACH TO BE TAKEN BY ONE PLATOON.

"A" COMPANY LANDED DIRECTLY UNDER THE GUNS OF THE GERMAN DEFENDERS. THEY IMMEDIATELY BEGIN TO MOVE TO SUPPRESS THE FIRE.

MOVE IT MEN!

AAARRGGH!

THEY ARE COVERED BY THE TANKS OF THE 1ST HUSSARS.

27

THE MEN OF CANADA'S QUEEN'S OWN RIFLES, LED BY LT. W. G. HERBERT, HAVE A MUCH HARDER TIME. TIDE AND WIND HAVE TAKEN THEM 200 YARDS EAST OF THEIR PLANNED LANDING -- AND RIGHT INTO THE FIRE OF THE GERMAN GUNS IN THE VILLAGE OF BERNIERES.

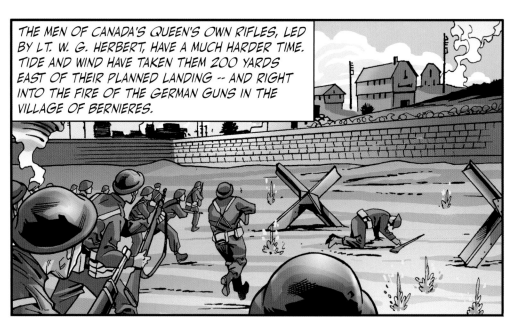

TRAPPED UNDER HEAVY FIRE, MAN AFTER MAN DROP INTO THE BOILING SURF.

LT. HERBERT KNOWS THAT SOMETHING HAS TO BE DONE QUICKLY OR THE BEACHHEAD WILL BE LOST.

HE, LANCE-CORPORAL RENE TESSIER, AND RIFLEMAN WILL CHICOSKI BREAK FOR THE SEAWALL...

ONCE THERE, THEY ARE ABLE TO USE ITS TEN-FOOT HEIGHT FOR COVER AS THEY INCH TOWARD THE GERMAN STRONGPOINT...

THEY ARE ABLE TO DESTROY THE GERMANS INSIDE.

FOR THEIR ACTION, ALL THREE MEN ARE AWARDED THE LEGION OF MERIT.*

*THE LEGION OF MERIT IS AWARDED TO U.S. ARMED FORCES FOR EXCEPTIONAL MILITARY ACTIONS.

THE ACTIONS OF THESE MEN AND OTHERS LIKE THEM HELP MOST OF THE TWO LEADING REGIMENTS SAFELY ASHORE AND READY TO MOVE INLAND.

THE GERMANS HAD LAID ABOUT 14,000 MINES BETWEEN COURSEULLES AND BERNIERES. BUT ALLIED ENGINEERS WORK TO CLEAR THE WAY, MAKING GAPS TO HELP TROOPS BEGIN TO MOVE INLAND...

...OFF THE BEACH, AND INTO FRANCE.

AT GOLD BEACH, THE BRITISH BEGIN THEIR OWN ATTACK.

GERMAN FIRE IS HEAVY, BUT NOTHING LIKE THAT ON OMAHA BEACH. BRITISH TROOPS QUICKLY GET OFF THE BEACH AND ONTO HIGHER GROUND.

SEEING HIS MEN PINNED DOWN BY MACHINE-GUN FIRE, SGT. MAJOR HOLLIS OF THE GREEN HOWARDS LAUNCHES AN IMMEDIATE ASSAULT.

HOLLIS HATES THE GERMANS. AT DUNKIRK,* HE HAD SEEN THE BODIES OF FRENCH MEN, WOMEN, AND CHILDREN KILLED BY THE NAZIS.

*DUNKIRK IS A FRENCH CITY, THAT WAS THE SITE OF HEAVY FIGHTING IN 1940.

EVER SINCE, HE HAD BECOME A HUNTER OF THE ENEMY.

WITHIN MINUTES, HE DESTROYS THE PILLBOX, KILLING THE TWO GERMAN SOLDIERS WHO WERE OPERATING THE MACHINE GUN.

SOON AFTER, HE IS INSTRUMENTAL IN THE CAPTURE OF A LARGE NUMBER OF GERMAN SOLDIERS WHO ARE SUPPORTING THE MACHINE GUN.

LATER THAT DAY, HOLLIS ATTACKS A GERMAN FIELD GUN AND SAVES TWO MEN TRAPPED BY ITS FIRE. HE WAS AWARDED THE VICTORIA CROSS -- THE ONLY WINNER OF THAT DECORATION ON D-DAY.

AT LA RIVIERE, THE EAST YORKSHIRE DIVISION IS UNDER HEAVY FIRE. THEY HAVE CALLED FOR NAVAL SUPPORT.

HEAVY SHELLING FORCES THE GERMANS TO DUCK FOR COVER.

THE 88MM WEAPON IS SOON SILENCED AND 45 GERMAN PRISONERS ARE TAKEN.

IT TAKES SEVERAL HOURS OF HOUSE-TO-HOUSE FIGHTING TO CLEAR THE VILLAGE, BUT IN THAT TIME THE ENTIRE AREA WAS TAKEN, ALLOWING THE BRITISH COLUMN TO ADVANCE TOWARD VER SUR MER.

GOLD BEACH IS SECURE.

LT. COLONEL JAMES RUDDER'S THREE RANGER COMPANIES HAVE BEEN ORDERED TO DESTROY THE LARGE COASTAL ARTILLERY CANNONS BETWEEN OMAHA AND UTAH BEACHES THAT MENACE THE AMERICAN BEACHES ON EITHER SIDE.

BUT DELAYED BY A NAVIGATION ERROR, THEY ARE LATE -- AND THE GERMANS ARE READY FOR THEM.

SOME MEN DO NOT WAIT FOR THE ROPES AND BEGIN CLIMBING BY HAND.

OTHERS, LIKE PRIVATE FIRST CLASS (PVC) HARRY ROBERTS, HAVE ALREADY HAD ROPES CUT TWO AND THREE TIMES.

SGT. BILL PETTY, ON HIS WAY UP FOR THE THIRD TIME, WATCHES AS A SOLDIER TO HIS RIGHT IS HIT BY GERMAN GUNFIRE.

DESPERATE, PETTY AND HIS COMRADES REACH THE TOP...

SCRAMBLING FOR COVER FROM THE GERMAN FIRE...

ONCE OVER THE EDGE OF THE CLIFF, THE RANGERS ARE ABLE TO FINISH THE LAST GERMAN DEFENDERS.

TRAINING COMES INTO PLAY AS SGT. PETTY, PVC ROBERTS, AND OTHER SURVIVING RANGERS MOVE FORWARD TOWARD THEIR TARGET.

UNTIL, EVENTUALLY, THEY GET INTO POSITION FOR THE FINAL ASSAULT...

THE MEN ARE FEARFUL OF THE DREADED POINTE DU HOC DEFENSES.*

*GERMAN FIELD MARSHAL ERWIN ROMMEL HAS FORTIFICATIONS WITH HEAVY ARTILLERY (POINTE DU HOC GUNS) BUILT ON THE CLIFFS AROUND THE BEACHES. THE ALLIES KNEW THEY WOULD BE DIFFICULT TO BEAT.

SGT. PETTY AND HIS MEN ARRIVE AT THE BUNKERS. THEY FIND NO GUNS.

TWO HOURS LATER A PATROL FINDS FIVE BIG GUNS AND AMMUNITION A FEW MILES AWAY. THE POINTE DU HOC GUNS THAT ROMMEL HAD ORDERED HAD NEVER BEEN PUT IN PLACE.

AS TROOPS MOVE INLAND FROM UTAH, SWORD, GOLD AND JUNO BEACHES, THOSE AT OMAHA ARE STILL PINNED DOWN. THEY ARE CAUGHT BETWEEN THE SEA AND THE HEAVY FIRE OF THE GERMAN DEFENDERS.

THINGS ARE SO BAD THAT AMERICAN GENERAL OMAR BRADLEY IS THINKING ABOUT GIVING UP AND PULLING THE TROOPS BACK FROM OMAHA BEACH.

BUT GENERAL NORMAN COTA IS NOT READY TO GIVE UP...

STRIDING THROUGH THE RAIN OF FIRE, HE ORDERS A GROUP OF RANGERS TO LEAD THE WAY OFF THE BEACH...

WHO KNOWS HOW TO DRIVE THIS THING?

I'LL DO IT, SIR.

ALL RIGHT! LET'S MOVE IT!

COTA LEADS BY EXAMPLE -- AND THE MEN OF OMAHA BEACH BEGIN TO FOLLOW HIM.

IT IS THE BEGINNING OF THE BREAKTHROUGH.

NOT FAR AWAY, A SECOND LEADER STEPS FORWARD. COLONEL CHARLES D. CANHAM, COMMANDER OF THE 116TH.

THEY'RE MURDERING US HERE!

LET'S MOVE INLAND AND GET MURDERED!

MEN LOSE THEIR FEAR AS THEIR LEADERS TAKE COMMAND OF THE SITUATION.

ONCE MOVING, THEY DO NOT STOP.

AS THEY MOVE, THE SECOND AND THIRD WAVES OF LANDING TROOPS COME IN. THE BOTTLE-NECK ON THE BEACH IS FINALLY BROKEN.

AS THE ALLIED FORCES BEGIN TO MAKE THEIR WAY OFF THE BEACHES, THE GERMANS FINALLY BEGIN TO REACT. GENERAL ERICH MARCKS KNEW THAT IF THE BRITISH CAPTURED CAEN, ALL WOULD BE LOST...

IF YOU DON'T SUCCEED IN THROWING THE BRITISH BACK INTO THE SEA, WE SHALL HAVE *LOST THE WAR!*

I HAVE TWO BATTALIONS, SIR. I WILL DO WHAT I CAN!

MOST GERMAN TANKS INSIDE FRANCE WERE UNDER THE DIRECT COMMAND OF ADOLF HITLER'S HEADQUARTERS. ONLY A VERY FEW WERE AVAILABLE FOR THE DEFENSE OF NORMANDY.

THOSE FEW BEGAN TO ROLL TOWARD THE BEACHES.

UNFORTUNATELY FOR THE GERMANS, LT. COLONEL MAURICE OF THE 2ND KINGS SHROPSHIRE LIGHT INFANTRY HAD BEEN ALERTED TO THEIR MOVEMENTS.

HURRY UP! LINE UP RIGHT HERE! THEY'LL HAVE TO COME THROUGH US TO REACH THE BEACHES!

AS PREDICTED, THE GERMAN FORCE CAME STRAIGHT AT THE CAREFULLY PLACED ANTITANK WEAPONS.

OPEN FIRE!

THE GERMAN ARMOR WAS MET BY A HAIL OF FIRE.

FOUR TANKS WERE IMMEDIATELY KNOCKED OUT.

THE OTHERS VEERED TO THE LEFT...

...WHERE THEY MET THE STAFFORDSHIRE YEOMANRY'S 17-POUND GUNS.

THE ADVANCE IS STOPPED BEFORE IT CAN REACH THE MEN ON THE BEACHES.

BACK AT THE KEY BRIDGES OVER THE CAEN RIVER, MAJOR HOWARD CONTINUES TO HOLD.

BUT HIS RESOURCES ARE RUNNING THIN AND HIS MEN GROWING TIRED.

I THINK I HEAR BAGPIPES!

YOU'RE DAFT!

NO! LOOK! THEY'RE HERE!

IT IS THE FIRST OF MANY LINKUPS BETWEEN THE AIRBORNE TROOPS AND THEIR COMRADES FROM THE BEACHES...

...AN INDICATION THAT THE INVASION HAS SUCCEEDED!

I WAS RIGHT ALL ALONG.

ALL ALONG...

DO YOU KNOW, IF I WAS COMMANDER OF THE ALLIED FORCES I COULD FINISH OFF THE WAR IN FOURTEEN DAYS.

AS NIGHT FALLS ON OMAHA BEACH, GENERAL NORMAN COTA GAZES AT THE SURF.

HE FINDS HIMSELF VERY TIRED.

BUT THERE IS NO TIME FOR REST NOW.

RUN ME UP THE HILL, SON.

AS GENERAL COTA REJOINS HIS TROOPS, SGT. ALFRED EIGENBERG, A MEDIC, TAKES A BREAK.

HE HAS LOST COUNT OF THE NUMBER OF WOUNDED HE HAS TREATED SINCE HIS LEAKING BOAT MADE IT TO SHORE.

HE IS BONE TIRED -- BUT THERE IS ONE THING HE MUST DO BEFORE HE SLEEPS...

Dear Mom and Dad.

By now you've heard of the invasion...

Well, I'm all right...

THE END.

THE BEGINNING OF THE END

The invasion of Normandy and the opening of a second front in Europe was the greatest disaster Hitler and the German Army had ever experienced. Aside from the presence of attacking Allied forces in Europe, it also cut the Germans off from the French Atlantic ports. This also meant an end to the German U-Boat war in the Atlantic.

Worse, the loss of the French coast deprived the Luftwaffe of their early warning radar systems, allowing Allied bombers easier access to the German cities. Later, as French airfields were captured, it also meant full-time Allied fighter bombings, and support for their troops.

German infantrymen captured by the Allies on D-Day were taken to prisoner of war camps in England. Most were between 18 and 19 years old. (NARA)

▼

▲

Once the Allies captured French airfields, they began full-time bombings of German troops across France and Germany. This destruction of resources helped lead to the end for Germany. (IWM)

As the Allies advanced through France, the Russians broke through more enemy lines and began a succession of attacks into the eastern flank of the German Reich.

German industry, bombed by the Allies and denied resources by the loss of key areas, began to falter. France had provided more than half the food needed by the German armies— as the Allies took back France these supplies were lost to the Germans. The loss of other French resources meant that much-needed weapons and equipment were not delivered quickly enough to the frontline units.

The German army began to retreat, contracting their defensive lines until they stood on the banks of the Rhine itself. By early 1945, Allied bombers were smashing through the German railway system, cutting off food and supplies to the interior of the country. Soon after, the Allied armies moved into German territory both from the east and the west. By April 25, Russian and American troops had met in several parts of Germany. The war was lost and, on April 30, Adolf Hitler committed suicide.

It had taken just 10 months from the first moment the first Allied troops touched the ground in occupied France until Germany surrendered. The war in Europe was over.

The final collapse of Germany happened once American and Soviet forces met each other in central Germany on April 21, 1945. (AKG Berlin)

▼

GLOSSARY

allies People or countries that give support to each other.

amphibious Coordinated land, sea and air forces organized for invasion.

artillery Large guns that are mounted.

assault A military attack that involves direct fighting.

bail To remove water from a boat by using a container to scoop up and throw the water overboard.

battalion A large group of military troops.

bombardment An attack that of heavy gunfire.

deployment To arange a military unit, especially to a wide position.

diligent Steady, energetic effort.

emplacement A place that has been prepared by the military for weapons.

foothold Position usable as a base for further advance.

fortification A building created to defend or strengthen a place or position.

glider An aircraft similar to an airplane but without an engine.

hostilities A conflict between two parties which usually leads to warfare.

infantry The branch of an army trained to fight on foot.

instrumental Being a vital part of getting something done.

invasion The act of sending armed forces to another country in order to take it over.

liberation The act of setting someone or somewhere free.

mainland The largest land mass of a country or continent relative to surrounding islands.

marshland An area of wetland, or marsh.

medic A person trained to give emergency medical help.

meteorology A science that deals with the atmosphere and especially with weather and weather forecasting.

paratrooper A soldier trained to jump from an airplane.

reinforce To strengthen or support by additional assistance.

shelling Attacking with artillery.

spearhead The leading force in getting something done.

suppress To stop something from happening.

FOR MORE INFORMATION

ORGANIZATIONS

The National World War II Museum
945 Magazine Street,
New Orleans,
LA 70130
USA
001 (504) 527 6012
Website: http://www.ddaymuseum.org/

D-Day Museum
Clarence Esplanade,
Southsea
PO5 3NT
01144 23 9229 6905
Website: http://www.ddaymuseum.co.uk/

FOR FURTHER READING

Parry, Dan, *D-Day: The Dramatic Story of the World's Greatest Invasion*, BBC Books, 2004

Bowman, Martin, *Remembering D-Day: Personal Histories of Everyday Heroes*, HarperCollins, 2004

Richard Holmes. *The D-Day Experience: From Invasion to the Liberation of Paris.* London:Carlton Books, 2004

Bryan Perrett, *D-Day (My Story)*, Scholastic, 2004

Troops huddled inside their LCVP landing craft as they waited to land on Omaha Beach on the morning of D-Day. Each LCVP carried 31 infantrymen and one officer. German forces had already started attacking the beach and soon the fight to get inland would begin. (Howard Gerrard © Osprey Publishing)

▼

INDEX